Cat Mandalas & Painted Moments

ADULT COLORING BOOK WITH POETRY AND SELF-DISCOVERY

Aventuras De Viaje

Copyright SF Nonfiction Books © 2023

All Rights Reserved

No part of this document may be reproduced without written consent from the author.

www.SFNonfictionBooks.com

INTRODUCTION

Welcome to a world where whiskers meet wonder, where feline beauty intertwines with the magical allure of colors. This isn't just any coloring book—it's an escape, a sanctuary, and a celebration of the delicate and profound world of cats.

Mandalas, ancient symbols of wholeness and unity, are known to usher in a meditative state, promoting mindfulness, focus, and inner peace. Combining this with the therapeutic act of coloring helps foster creativity and provides a delightful respite from everyday stresses. Diving into this book, you're embracing not just an artistic endeavor, but also an exercise in introspection and mindfulness.

Taking time for ourselves in this fast-paced world is essential. Coloring allows us to pause, to immerse in the present moment, and to rekindle our relationship with our inner selves. It's about tapping into that childlike wonder we all hold inside and letting it gleam through colors.

Navigating the Feline-Inspired Pages

Dive deeper, and you'll find that this book has been meticulously crafted to enhance your personal journey:

- **Simple Activities:** Beyond just coloring, engage with activities designed to spark reflection and creativity. These gentle prompts will lead you to moments of introspection, serving as kindling for your inner fire.
- **Quotes:** Let the wisdom of personal development accompany you, illuminating your path as you add your own burst of color to the pages.
- **Positive Affirmations:** As you color, let these words of positivity uplift your spirit, molding your thoughts and inspiring a brighter perspective.
- **Poems and Haikus:** Revel in the poetic tales of felines and life's many dances. Each rhythm and every line, a muse for your artistic endeavors.

Embark on this coloring odyssey, immersing yourself in the world of cats and the therapeutic embrace of art.

THANKS FOR YOUR PURCHASE

Get Your Next SF Nonfiction Book FREE!

Claim the book of your choice at:

www.SFNonfictionBooks.com/Free-Book

You will also be among the first to know of all the latest releases, discount offers, bonus content, and more.

Go to:

www.SFNonfictionBooks.com/Free-Book

Thanks again for your support.

Daily Blessing:
What made you smile today?

_____

_____

"The best way to predict the future is to create it."
- Abraham Lincoln

I possess the qualities needed to be successful.

Whiskers twitch and gleam,
Silent paws in moonlit dreams,
Night's soft, feline beam.

Kindness Shown:
Write about a kind gesture you received today

_____

_____

"Growth and comfort do not coexist."
- Ginni Rometty

All my actions are aligned with my purpose.

Gentle roars from a distant past,
Echoes of a time so vast.
Through alleyways, ruins, and halls,
The feline spirit forever calls.

Kindness Given:
How did you make someone's day better?

_____

_____

"Becoming is better than being."
- Carol Dweck

Every day, I discover more of my potential.

Purring melodies,
Warmth nestled in gentle breeze,
Dreams as vast as seas.

Simple Pleasures:
List three little things you're grateful for today.

_____

_____

"The road to personal excellence has no end."
- Tarun Sharma

I am in charge of how I feel, and today I choose happiness.

Moonlit whiskers, a silent meow,
Timeless tales, here and now.
Wisdom carried on gentle paws,
Cats live by their own set of laws.

Golden Moment:
Reflect on a moment today that filled your heart.

_____

_____

"He who conquers himself is the mightiest warrior."
- Confucius

I am resilient, strong, and brave.

Feline grace, so pure,
In their gaze, a world's allure,
Mysteries endure.

**Gift of Time:
Who did you spend quality time with today?**

_____

_____

"The biggest room in the world is the room for improvement."
- Helmut Schmidt

My past does not define me; it only makes me wiser.

Journey onward, step by step,
Cherish memories, secrets kept.
In life's dance, twirl and sway,
Find your rhythm, come what may.

Nature's Bounty:
What beauty did you observe in nature today?

_____

_____

"Turn inward and apply your strength to yourself."
- Epictetus

I am worthy of all my dreams and aspirations.

Velvet paws tread light,
Dancing shadows in the night,
Eyes glowing so bright.

Unexpected Joy:
Share something that pleasantly surprised you.

_____

_____

"The only limit to our realization of tomorrow is our doubts of today."
- Franklin D. Roosevelt

I release all doubts and trust the process.

Elegant and sleek,
Mysteries they always seek,
Secrets cats do keep.

Caring for Others:
How did you show empathy or concern today?

_____

_____

"Life is a succession of lessons which must be lived to be understood."
- Ralph Waldo Emerson

Every challenge I face is an opportunity for growth.

Echoes of ancient tales resound,
In every leap and playful bound.
Stories of valor, love, and mirth,
Cats, the enchanters of the earth.

Warm Memories:
Reflect on a cherished memory
that came to mind.

_____

_____

"The most important investment you can make is in yourself."
- Warren Buffett

The world is full of endless possibilities and opportunities.

A leap, a chase, a playful prance,
In feline eyes, life's endless dance.
Grace and poise, wild and free,
The spirit of cats, for all to see.

Lessons Learned:
What challenge today are you grateful for?

_____

_____

"Our greatest freedom is the freedom to choose our attitude."
- Viktor E. Frankl

I trust the journey and believe in my path.

Silent, they observe,
Every move, every swerve,
Grace in every curve.

A Helping Hand:
How did you assist someone today?

_____

_____

"What lies behind us and what lies before us are tiny matters compared to what lies within us."
- Ralph Waldo Emerson

Challenges are opportunities for growth and improvement.

Eyes wide, tail aloft,
Mysteries in shadows soft,
Secrets whispered oft.

Tomorrow's Promise:
What are you looking forward to?

_____

_____

"The journey of a thousand miles begins with a single step."
- Lao Tzu

BEYOND THESE PAGES

A Deeper Dive into Art and Soul Awaits!

This book is but a chapter in a voyage where creativity meets depth.

Craving more? Explore the link below and weave deeper into the tapestry of art and emotion.

www.SFNonfictionBooks.com/Adult-Coloring-Books

A HEARTFELT THANK YOU

As the colors on these pages have come to life, so has our shared journey in this artistic realm. I am deeply grateful for your trust in choosing this book, and more so for allowing it to be a part of your self-care and personal journey.

Taking time for oneself is a gift—a silent promise of growth, introspection, and rejuvenation. By picking up the colors and filling these pages, you've not just created art but have also woven moments of peace, reflection, and creativity into your life.

Thank you for making space for yourself, for embracing the feline wonders, and for dancing to the rhythm of the lines and hues within this book. Your journey here is a testament to the beauty of dedicating time to one's soul and spirit.

If you enjoyed this journey and wish to explore more, know that there are other themes awaiting your artistic touch. Dive into new worlds and let your imagination flow.

From the deepest corner of my heart, thank you for bringing this book to life. Until our next artistic adventure together, cherish the colors of your journey and continue to shine.

Warmly,

Aventuras De Viaje

ABOUT THE AUTHOR

Aventuras has three passions: travel, writing, and learning new skills.

Combining these three things, Miss Viaje spends her time exploring the world and learning about anything and everything that interests her, from yoga, to music, to science, and more.

Aventuras takes what she discovers and shares it through her books.

www.SFNonfictionBooks.com

www.ingramcontent.com/pod-product-compliance
Lightning Source LLC
Chambersburg PA
CBHW081725100526
44591CB00016B/2510